ABOUT THE CREATOR
Queen Tasha

Queen Tasha is a creative visionary, nomadic entrepreneur, and founder of Crowned Consulting. In this soul-led brand, she is dedicated to helping women reclaim their power, live freely, and express their divine purpose without apology.

After years of personal transformation, from traditional living to full-time RV life and self-sovereignty, Queen Tasha learned that true freedom starts within. In the mind, in the heart, and in the daily choices we make to honor ourselves.

She created this Guide & Workbook as a roadmap for other queens who are ready to shift old patterns, rewrite outdated stories, and rise into the highest version of themselves. Guides like this have always been sacred tools in her own evolution, helping her organize her thoughts, track her growth, and stay grounded while following her calling. Now, she shares that same process with you so that you can walk your own royal path with clarity, confidence, and crown intact.

Remember: You are the author of your life; this guide is simply the mirror reminding you of your power.

TABLE OF CONTENT

1. How to Use This Workbook
2. Purpose of This Guide
3. The 6 Attributes of a Queen
   - Sovereignty
   - Discernment
   - Resilience
   - Grace
   - Patience
   - Discipline
4. Bonus: Rising Sign Oracle Messages
5. The Queen's Contract

HOW TO USE THIS WORKBOOK

This workbook is your sacred space of reflection, activation, and embodiment. Each chapter invites you to explore one of the Six Royal Attributes that form the foundation of a powerful Queen.

You'll read, reflect, write, affirm, and embody. Each section has:
- Meaning: Understand the essence of each attribute.
- Reflection: Receive insight into how it shows up in your life.
- Journal Prompts: Dive deep into self-awareness.
- Affirmation/Mantra: Anchor new beliefs.
- Embodiment Practice: Take spiritual principles into motion.
- Coloring Page: A meditative art ritual to soothe and integrate.

✦ This is a royal initiation back into your truth.

PURPOSE OF THIS GUIDE & WORKBOOK

This workbook is designed to accompany the Attributes of a Queen video series and group coaching experience, helping you deepen your connection with each quality through personal reflection and practice.

Whether you're part of the Queens Rising Collective or journeying solo through the Sovereign Queen Path, this guide will help you:

- Build a foundation of emotional, spiritual, and mental resilience.
- Reclaim your crown through daily embodiment.
- Anchor your new mindset and habits into everyday life.

This is your royal roadmap back to self-sovereignty.

THE 6 FOUNDATIONAL ATTRIBUTES OF A QUEEN

SOVEREIGNTY

DISCERNMENT

RESILIENCE

GRACE

PATIENCE

DISCIPLINE

🔑 General Definition

Sovereignty means supreme power, authority, and self-rule. It is the freedom to govern your own life and energy, standing in full ownership of your choices without apology or permission.

💎 Empowered Queen Meaning

For the Queen, sovereignty is divine authority. It is knowing that you are the ruler of your inner kingdom, mind, body, and spirit.
To live sovereignly means you are no longer guided by fear, approval, or control. You are led by intuition, integrity, and inner truth.
A sovereign Queen doesn't beg for power; she embodies it. She creates her reality through conscious decision, clear boundaries, and unwavering faith in her purpose.
You don't follow the system; you build your own throne within it.

📖 EXPANDED REFLECTION

- Sovereignty begins when you realize your life is yours to design.
- It is the reclamation of power once given away through people-pleasing, conformity, or fear.
- It is choosing to lead yourself with love instead of waiting to be chosen.
- Sovereignty is not dominance over others — it is mastery over self.
- It is your divine right to live by your own rhythm, values, and vision.

When you rise into sovereignty, you stop asking, "Who will let me?"
and start declaring, "Who can stop me?"

✨ Quotes on Sovereignty

"Emancipate yourselves from mental slavery; none but ourselves can free our minds."
— Bob Marley

"Your crown has been bought and paid for. Put it on your head and wear it."
— Maya Angelou

"The most common way people give up their power is by thinking they don't have any."
— Alice Walker

"When we are powerful, we are not followers, we are not going along with the social constructs, we are making our own rules, making our own life, being the ruler of our own life. You have to lead yourself, no matter what's going on."
— Queen Tasha

PRACTICAL WAYS TO EMBODY SOVEREIGNTY THIS WEEK

Freedom Freestyle Dance
- Choose a song or playlist that makes you feel limitless. Let your body move without choreography or judgment.
- Imagine shaking off the rules, expectations, and "shoulds" that have confined you.
- This is a ritual of reclamation, movement as rebellion and release.

Bonus: Record yourself and post on your socials

Break the Rule Practice
- Identify one rule, belief, or expectation you've been conditioned to follow but no longer agree with.
- Consciously and safely break it this week, not to rebel recklessly, but to reclaim your right to choose.
- This is your act of liberation from mental slavery.

Energy Sovereignty Audit
- Notice who or what drains you versus what nourishes you.
- Place your hands over your heart and say:

"I reclaim all energy that belongs to me. I release what is not mine."

- Visualize your power returning as golden light filling your aura.

Reflections from Embodiment Practices

Reflections from Embodiment Practices

Reflections from Embodiment Practices

👑 AFFIRMATION & MANTRA

Short Daily Affirmations:

- "I am the ruler of my life, guided by divine authority."
- "I rise in my truth, unshaken and unapologetic."
- "I embody freedom as my birthright and choice."

Long Mantra:

"I am the sovereign Queen of my own destiny.
 I release the need for external validation and reclaim my inner authority.
 My decisions are sacred, my boundaries are divine, and my energy is my throne.
 I move through life with purpose and power, knowing that I am fully equipped to lead myself.
 My Queendom is built on faith, freedom, and fierce self-trust.
 I reign with love, wisdom, and unwavering devotion to my highest self."
ASE'

JOURNALING PROMPTS:
What made you realize you were the co-creator of your life?

JOURNALING PROMPTS:
What beliefs or fears have kept you from standing in your full power?

JOURNALING PROMPTS:
Where in your life do you need to reclaim authority?

Journaling Prompts:
How do you define FREEDOM in Your Life?

Oracle Card Pull Reflection

Deck Name: _____

Card 1: _____

Oracle Card Pull Reflection

Deck Name: _____

Card 2:_____

Oracle Card Pull Reflection

Deck Name: _____

Card 3: _____

"I am the ruler of my own life,
Living Fearlessly Free!"

ATTRIBUTE 2: DISCERNMENT

🗝️ General Definition

Discernment is the ability to see clearly, to distinguish truth from illusion, alignment from distraction, and divine timing from delay. It is intuitive wisdom sharpened by experience and guided by faith.

💎 Empowered Queen Meaning

For a Queen, discernment is her royal intuition in motion. It's not just about making decisions — it's about seeing beyond the surface. Discernment allows you to know when to move, when to wait, and when to walk away. It's the crown jewel of wisdom that helps you protect your peace, energy, and kingdom.

A discerning Queen doesn't move in haste. She listens deeply, observes carefully, and acts from alignment — not ego. Her "no" is sacred. Her "yes" is powerful. Her silence is strategy.

📖 EXPANDED REFLECTION

- Discernment is clarity through the fog.
- It's the whisper of your higher self saying, "Trust what you feel."
- Every opportunity isn't for you. Every person doesn't deserve access to your energy.
- A Queen with discernment doesn't chase; she attracts through alignment.
- Discernment refines your intuition and protects your power.

✨ Quotes on Discernment

Yoruba Proverb
"The eyes that see clearly are guided by the heart that listens."

Oprah Winfrey
"Your life speaks to you in whispers. When you don't listen to the whisper, it comes as a shout."

Iyanla Vanzant
"Discernment is not judgment — it's clarity. It's how you honor your truth without condemning another's."

Maya Angelou
"When someone shows you who they are, believe them — the first time."

PRACTICAL WAYS TO EMBODY DISCERNMENT THIS WEEK

Intuitive Body Scanning
- Sit in silence and bring awareness from your crown to your toes.
- Ask your body about any major decision you have coming up?
- Notice sensations tension, warmth, chills, gut reaction, this is your body's way of speaking truth.
- What decision is your body calling you to make?

Reprogramming the Mind
- Each time confusion or doubt arises, place your hand on your third eye and repeat:
- "I see truth with clarity and compassion."
- Breathe slowly until your nervous system relaxes — clarity cannot exist in chaos.
- Write down any intuitive messages that surface during or after this practice.

Silent Thought Practice:
- Spend 5–10 minutes daily in stillness and silence because clarity loves quiet. (no need to meditate)
- Take this time to just let thoughts flow in, say yes or now, and let them flow out.
- Don't spend too much time on the thought; just make a quick decision to return to silence.

Reflections from Embodiment Practices

Reflections from Embodiment Practices

Reflections from Embodiment Practices

👑 AFFIRMATION & MANTRA

Short Versions:
- "I trust my intuition. My inner voice is wise and clear."
- "I move with clarity and confidence. My discernment is divine."

Long Mantra:
"I rise as the Queen of clarity, guided by divine discernment.
My intuition is my compass, my peace is my power.
I do not rush — I trust.
I release confusion, manipulation, and fear.
I see truth in all things and alignment in all choices.
I move with wisdom, intuition, and royal grace.
What is meant for me flows with ease, and what is not falls away with peace."
ASE'

JOURNALING PROMPTS:
When have you ignored your intuition, and what did you learn from it?

JOURNALING PROMPTS:
How does Intuition feel in your body when it speaks?

JOURNALING PROMPTS:
Who or what has challenged your discernment lately? How did you respond?

Oracle Card Pull Reflection

Deck Name: _____

Card 1: _____

Oracle Card Pull Reflection

Deck Name: _____

Card 2: _____

Oracle Card Pull Reflection

Deck Name: _____
Card 3: _____

"I trust my intuition to guide me with clarity."

ATTRIBUTE 3: RESILIENCE

🗝️ General Definition

Resilience is the capacity to recover, adapt, and rise stronger after life's storms. It's the unbreakable thread of strength that connects your past, present, and divine purpose.

💎 Empowered Queen Meaning

For a Queen, resilience is sacred endurance — the knowing that no challenge can take her crown.

It's not about pretending everything is fine. It's about acknowledging the pain, feeling it fully, and still choosing to rise.

Resilience is the spiritual muscle built through surrender, self-trust, and divine faith.

Every fall teaches grace. Every setback sharpens strength. Every ending reveals rebirth. A resilient Queen doesn't just survive — she transforms.

📖 EXPANDED REFLECTION

- Resilience is not about avoiding challenges, but embracing them as teachers.
- A Queen recognizes that every obstacle is an initiation into deeper strength and grace.
- Your ability to withstand, adapt, and grow is proof that you are unshakable, even when the world tries to break you.
- Resilience is also patience — trusting divine timing and understanding that healing, rebuilding, and thriving take time.

✨ Quotes on Resilience

"You may encounter many defeats, but you must not be defeated."
— Maya Angelou

"Do not judge me by my success, judge me by how many times I fell down and got back up again."
— Nelson Mandela

"If you fall, fall on your back. If you can look up, you can get up. Let your reason get you back up."
— Les Brown

PRACTICAL WAYS TO EMBODY RESILIENCE THIS WEEK

Dragon Breath Practice
- Sit tall. Inhale deeply through your nose, imagining yourself going through life's toughest challenges
- Exhale forcefully through the mouth with audible growl, visualizing the release of pain, fear, frustration or past burdens.
- Repeat 7 times, saying inwardly: "I rise renewed."
- Feel your body expand with each breath, reminding you that rebirth is your nature.

Workout Challenge
- Find a 5-7 day fitness challenge on YouTube that is new to you.
- Push yourself to complete each move even when its hard.
- By the end of the challenge, try to do an advanced version of the moves to push yourself past your limits.
- Fitness challenges teach us the power of pain and resilience.

Reflections from Embodiment Practices

Reflections from Embodiment Practices

Reflections from Embodiment Practices

👑 AFFIRMATION & MANTRA

Short:

- "I am resilient. Every challenge refines me, strengthens me, and reminds me that I am unshakable.
- "I rise again and again — softer, wiser, stronger."

Long:

"I honor the parts of me that have fallen and risen countless times.

I trust that every test refines my purpose and strengthens my throne.

I am the living embodiment of resilience — the Queen who bends but never breaks.

My faith is my fortress, and my healing is my revolution."

JOURNALING PROMPTS:

Reflect on a moment when life tested you recently.
How did you feel in the midst of the challenge?

JOURNALING PROMPTS:

Reflect on a moment when life tested you recently.
What inner resources did you call on to keep going?

_____
_____
_____
_____
_____
_____
_____
_____
_____
_____
_____
_____
_____
_____
_____
_____
_____

JOURNALING PROMPTS:

Reflect on a moment when life tested you recently. What did it teach you about your strength?

Oracle Card Pull Reflection

Deck Name: _____

Card 1: _____

Oracle Card Pull Reflection

Deck Name: _____
Card 2: _____

Oracle Card Pull Reflection

Deck Name: _____

Card 3: _____

"From every fall, I rise like a Phoenix,
fierce and stronger."

ATTRIBUTE 4: GRACE

🗝 General Definition

Grace is simple elegance or refinement of movement; courteous goodwill. It is the quality of moving through life with poise, kindness, and effortless dignity.

💎 Empowered Queen Meaning

For a Queen, Grace is not just about appearance or politeness; it's a sacred energy. Grace is the way you extend compassion to yourself and others, the way you rise above pettiness, and the way you remain rooted in love no matter the chaos around you.

Grace does not mean weakness; it is strength under control. A Queen walks in grace because she knows her worth, honors her boundaries, and carries her crown lightly but firmly.

📖 EXPANDED REFLECTION

- Grace is strength wrapped in softness.
- It is not about perfection, but presence.
- Grace is choosing peace over ego
- Grace allows us to walk away without resentment, speak truth without cruelty, and love without losing ourselves.
- A Queen who leads with grace leads with light.

✨ QUOTES ON GRACE

"Grace means that all of your mistakes now serve a purpose instead of serving shame."
— Brene Brown

Courage is grace under pressure.
— Ernest Hemingway

"When they go low, we go high."
— Michelle Obama

"I do not at all understand the mystery of grace - only that it meets us where we are but does not leave us where it found us."
— Anne Lamott

🌹 PRACTICAL WAYS TO EMBODY GRACE THIS WEEK

Main Character Energy Walk
- Go for a walk in nature or around your neighborhood, or model walk down the hallway.
- Walk with your chin slightly lifted, shoulders back, and light on your toes as if you are gliding, with the confidence of a well-paid supermodel
- Changing the way you walk allows Grace to mature without ego.

Radical Forgiveness Letter
- Write a letter of forgiveness — to yourself or someone else.
- You don't need to send it. Simply allow the energy to release from your body onto the page.
- Burn or bury the letter, saying: "I free myself from the weight of what was."

Water Blessing Ritual
- As you shower or bathe, imagine the water cleansing not just your body but your emotional field.
- Whisper: "I am washed in love, renewed in grace."
- Feel tension dissolve, replaced by a lightness that lingers long after.

Reflections from Embodiment Practices

Reflections from Embodiment Practices

Reflections from Embodiment Practices

👑 AFFIRMATION & MANTRA

Short:

- "I move with ease, flow, and divine grace."
- "I forgive, release, and rise in love."

Long:

"I embody grace in every breath, every word, every motion.

I choose compassion where I once chose control.

I surrender what is not mine to carry and release what no longer serves my peace.

I am both gentle and powerful, a living reflection of divine grace."

"I walk with confidence as the main character of my story."

JOURNALING PROMPTS:

Where in your life can you give yourself more grace?

JOURNALING PROMPTS:
Who in your life deserves more grace?

JOURNALING PROMPTS:
When Challenged: What would it look like to respond with grace instead?

ORACLE CARD PULL REFLECTION

Deck Name: _____

Card 1: _____

Oracle Card Pull Reflection

Deck Name: _____
Card 2: _____

ORACLE CARD PULL REFLECTION

Deck Name: _____

Card 3: _____

"I move with ease, beauty, and divine flow."

ATTRIBUTE 5: PATIENCE

🔑 General Definition

Patience is the ability to accept delay, obstacles, and divine timing without losing faith or alignment.

💎 Empowered Queen Meaning

For a Queen, patience is not passive — it's a powerful practice of trust. Patience is knowing that what is meant for you cannot miss you, and that rushing the process only robs you of the lessons along the way.

Patience is strength in stillness, the discipline of waiting without worry, and the quiet confidence that your crown is secure, even in seasons of delay.

📖 EXPANDED REFLECTION

- Patience teaches us that delay is not denial, it's divine preparation.
- Patience is not weakness; it is the deep knowing that all things unfold in perfect timing.
- Patience teaches us that not every season is for action; some are for planting, resting, and allowing the soil to do its sacred work.
- A Queen understands that her growth, her healing, and her blessings cannot be rushed.
- Patience requires trust, in yourself, in others, and in the Spirit.
- True patience allows us to release control and embrace peace in the waiting.

✨ Quotes on Patience

"We spend precious hours fearing the inevitable. It would be wise to use that time adoring our families, cherishing our friends, and living our lives."
—Maya Angelou

"Nature has no agenda. The grass doesn't rush to grow, the sun doesn't rush to rise. Yet all of it happens in perfect timing."
—Oprah Winfrey

"Patience is not simply the ability to wait — it's how we behave while we're waiting."

Jean-Jacques Rousseau
"Patience is bitter, but its fruit is sweet"
—Joyce Meyer

🌹 PRACTICAL WAYS TO EMBODY PATIENCE THIS WEEK

Intermittent Fasting:
- If you are used to eating breakfast first thing in the morning when you rise, I challenge you for the next 7 days to wait to eat.
- Intermittent Fasting is proven to have miraculous health benefits for numerous reasons, but is also a practice for patients.
- This patient allows your body to fully complete the digestion process before starting the next cycle.
- Have a hot beverage and water with lemon; this will help prepare your body as well as curb your appetite.
- Set your breakfast time 12-16 hours after your last meal.

Nature Timing:
- Spend time observing something natural, a sunrise or sunset 1 hour before, a flower opening for the morning, a tide, or a stream as water flows.
- Let it teach you how beauty unfolds without haste.

Chat with a child or an elder:
1. Ask a child or an elder to tell you a story or explain their POV on an important topic, and JUST LISTEN!
2. It takes a lot of patience to allow someone to speak and just listen, especially with a child or an elder.

Reflections from Embodiment Practices

Reflections from Embodiment Practices

Reflections from Embodiment Practices

👑 AFFIRMATION & MANTRA

Short Mantras:
- "I am patient, poised, and aligned with divine timing."
- "What's meant for me cannot be rushed; it's already mine in spirit."

Long Mantra:

"I honor the sacred pace of my becoming.
I release the need to force or control outcomes.
With every breath, I align with divine flow and perfect timing.
In patience, I find peace.
In surrender, I find strength.
I am not waiting, I am preparing.
I am becoming everything I am meant to be."

JOURNALING PROMPTS:

How do you react when things don't move as fast as you'd like, and what does that reveal about your trust in the process?

JOURNALING PROMPTS:

Where in your life are you being asked to slow down and trust divine timing?

JOURNALING PROMPTS:

How can you cultivate peace in the waiting period?

JOURNALING PROMPTS:

What have you learned from seasons of waiting or delay?

Oracle Card Pull Reflection

Deck Name: _____
Card 1: _____

ORACLE CARD PULL REFLECTION

Deck Name: _____
Card 2: _____

Oracle Card Pull Reflection

Deck Name: _____
Card 3: _____

"I trust the divine timing, waiting in peace."

ATTRIBUTE 6: DISCIPLINE

🗝 General Definition

Discipline is the practice of training oneself to act with consistency, focus, and self-control in pursuit of a higher vision. It's not punishment, but the structure that allows freedom and growth.

💎 Empowered Queen Meaning

For a Queen, discipline is sacred devotion. It is the commitment to your values, your healing, your growth, your dreams, and your reign. Discipline is the quiet force that turns intentions into reality.

It's not about perfection or cruelty to oneself; it's about showing up daily, even when you don't feel like it. A Queen's discipline is how she proves to herself that her vision matters, her purpose is worth it, and her legacy is alive in her every choice.

Discipline is devotion in action.

📖 EXPANDED REFLECTION

- Discipline is self-love in practice.
- Discipline is consistency that crowns you, brick by brick, day by day.
- It is devotion to your higher self, not punishment of your present self.
- Without discipline, even the greatest vision will fade.
- With discipline, the Queen builds, sustains, and reigns in power.

✨ Quotes on Discipline

"Without commitment, you'll never start. But more importantly, without consistency, you'll never finish."
— Denzel Washington

"Forget inspiration. Habit is more dependable. Habit will sustain you whether you're inspired or not."
— Octavia Butler

"Dreams are built on discipline; discipline is built on habits; habits are built on training."
— Will Smith

"Enthusiasm is common. Endurance is rare."
— Angela Duckworth

PRACTICAL WAYS TO EMBODY DISCIPLINE THIS WEEK

Mirror Devotion:
- Stand before your mirror, place your hand on your heart, and speak your long mantra aloud.
- Feel the vibration of your words as a royal decree.

Learn Something New:
- Learn a new skill or information that will benefit you for the next step in a big goal you have.
- Use YouTube University or a free learning platform.
- Don't make it complicated. Knowledge is power.

Habit Tracking:
- Use the Grid Below to track up to 3 habits that you have a hard time remembering to do, but are important to you. (i.e, taking vitamins, drinking water, going for a walk, reading a book page, etc.)
- Set a reward if you accomplish all habits after 7 days

	S	M	T	W	T	F	S
_____	☐	☐	☐	☐	☐	☐	☐
_____	☐	☐	☐	☐	☐	☐	☐
_____	☐	☐	☐	☐	☐	☐	☐
_____	☐	☐	☐	☐	☐	☐	☐
_____	☐	☐	☐	☐	☐	☐	☐
_____	☐	☐	☐	☐	☐	☐	☐

Reflections from Embodiment Practices

Reflections from Embodiment Practices

Reflections from Embodiment Practices

👑 AFFIRMATION & MANTRA

Short Mantras:
- "I honor my discipline as devotion."
- "My consistency crowns me."

Long Mantra:

"I honor my discipline as devotion to my highest good.

Each choice I make builds the empire of my dreams.

Through consistency and commitment, I crown myself daily.

I move with alignment, focus, and royal purpose,

knowing that every brick I lay strengthens my Queendom.

Discipline is not restriction; it is my roadmap to freedom."

JOURNALING PROMPTS:

Where in your life do you crave more consistency, and what's blocking you from it?

JOURNALING PROMPTS:

How would your reality shift if you treated discipline as devotion to yourself?

JOURNALING PROMPTS:

What is something you say you can't do?
Ask yourself why.

JOURNALING PROMPTS:

What "Empire" are you currently building through your daily choices & habits?

Oracle Card Pull Reflection

Deck Name: _____

Card 1: _____

Oracle Card Pull Reflection

Deck Name: _____

Card 2: _____

Oracle Card Pull Reflection

Deck Name: _____

Card 3: _____

*"Through consistency and devotion,
I build my Queendom."*

BONUS SECTION:
Rising Sign Oracle Messages

Why Your Rising Sign Matters More Than Your Sun Sign

When reading this section, I invite you to focus on your Rising Sign (Ascendant) rather than your Sun sign.

Your Rising Sign represents the lens through which you experience the world—how your soul shows up in human form, how you respond to life's lessons, and how you integrate growth in your body, mind, and spirit. While your Sun sign speaks to your essence, your Rising Sign reveals the journey your essence is here to embody.

In the context of the Queens Rising journey, your Rising Sign reflects how your inner Queen rises—how you express sovereignty, discernment, resilience, grace, patience, and discipline through your unique soul design. Read your Rising Sign message as a personal oracle transmission, guiding you toward deeper embodiment of your regal power.

Rising Sign Oracle Messages

♈ **Aries Rising – The Initiating Queen**
You rise through bold action and fearless beginnings. Sovereignty for you is saying "yes" to your fire without waiting for permission. Practice discernment by pausing before reacting—your power multiplies through patience. Remember: leadership is not about domination but divine direction.

♉ **Taurus Rising – The Grounded Queen**
You rise through stability, sensuality, and sacred comfort. Sovereignty begins when you realize your worth is not tied to productivity. Discern what truly nourishes your spirit and release attachments that create stagnation. Rebuild your resilience by rooting in beauty and peace, not in resistance.

♊ **Gemini Rising – The Messenger Queen**
You rise through expression and curiosity. Sovereignty means trusting your voice as sacred truth. Discernment for you is knowing when to speak and when silence carries more power. Grace flows when you communicate from alignment, not anxiety. Let your words be spells of clarity and connection.

♋ **Cancer Rising – The Nurturing Queen**
You rise through emotion, care, and intuitive wisdom. Sovereignty is reclaiming your sensitivity as your superpower. Strengthen your resilience by creating emotional safety within yourself before seeking it externally. Grace for you is in receiving as much as you give.

♌ **Leo Rising – The Radiant Queen**
You rise through self-expression and joy. Sovereignty means shining without apology. Practice discernment by aligning your spotlight with purpose, not validation. Your resilience lies in your ability to rise again in love, even after rejection. Your throne is your heart—rule from there.

♍ **Virgo Rising – The Devoted Queen**
You rise through service, integrity, and refinement. Sovereignty means owning your sacred standards while releasing perfectionism. Discernment for you is knowing what truly requires fixing and what deserves flow. Grace is your ability to turn every detail into devotion.

Rising Sign Oracle Messages

♎ **Libra Rising – The Harmonizing Queen**
You rise through beauty, balance, and relationships. Sovereignty is remembering that peace is an inside job. Discernment is choosing reciprocity over people-pleasing. Stand tall in your boundaries; your grace is magnetic when you honor your own reflection first.

♏ **Scorpio Rising – The Transformative Queen**
You rise through depth, power, and rebirth. Sovereignty is your ability to release control and still trust the process. Discernment means reading energy beyond words. You embody resilience like no other—each ending is a resurrection. Your grace is forged in shadow and emerges as gold.

♐ **Sagittarius Rising – The Visionary Queen**
You rise through truth, freedom, and expansion. Sovereignty is claiming your own belief system and walking it boldly. Discernment means knowing when exploration becomes escapism. Resilience for you is found in faith—grace is your laughter after every fall.

♑ **Capricorn Rising – The Sovereign Queen**
You rise through mastery, structure, and wisdom. Sovereignty is not earned—it's embodied through responsibility and self-trust. Discernment for you is learning the difference between control and authority. Grace flows when you soften into your own timing.

♒ **Aquarius Rising – The Revolutionary Queen**
You rise through innovation, individuality, and service to the collective. Sovereignty means honoring your uniqueness even when it defies tradition. Discernment for you is knowing which systems to reform and which to leave behind. Grace comes through authenticity—your presence is permission for others to be free.

♓ **Pisces Rising – The Mystic Queen**
You rise through empathy, imagination, and surrender. Sovereignty means owning your energetic sensitivity as divine intelligence. Discernment is trusting your intuition over illusion. Resilience comes from faith in the unseen; grace flows through your connection to Source.

THE QUEEN'S CONTRACT: SACRED SOVEREIGNTY PLEDGE

This is your moment to anchor everything you've learned — to declare, in your own words, your devotion to the Queen you are becoming.

The Queen's Contract is a sacred agreement between your current self and your highest self. It represents your readiness to rise in truth, love, and divine authority. By signing your name, you proclaim that you are reclaiming your crown — not as a symbol of control, but as a reminder of your divine birthright to live freely, fully, and fearlessly. Take a moment to breathe deeply. Place your hand over your heart and feel the rhythm of your own kingdom within.

THE QUEEN'S CONTRACT: SACRED SOVEREIGNTY PLEDGE

I, _____,

do hereby reclaim my throne within.

I choose to live as a Sovereign Queen — guided by my intuition, grounded in my truth, and devoted to my evolution.

I release all vows of limitation, fear, and unworthiness.

I honor my discernment as divine guidance.

I cultivate resilience through faith and grace.

I embody patience as sacred timing.

I practice discipline as devotion to my higher purpose.

From this day forward, I vow to walk in alignment with love, to lead with compassion, and to remember that I am never separate from Source.

My crown is remembered.

My power is reclaimed.

My reign is over my own energy, mind, and destiny.

With an open heart and steady spirit,

I sign this contract in full awareness of my divinity.

✨ Signature: _____

✨ Date: _____

YOU WERE BORN A QUEEN NOW IT'S TIME TO RISE!

www.ingramcontent.com/pod-product-compliance
Lightning Source LLC
Chambersburg PA
CBHW051353070526
44584CB00025B/3746